GU00891797

Test your

Potential

BRIAN O'NEILL AND LIZ O'NEILL

Series editors: GARETH LEWIS & GENE CROZIER

Hodder & Stoughton

A MEMBER OF THE HODDER HEADLINE GROUP

Dedicated to:

Nan Loudon, the strength in the family, and Alan Paivio, friend and mentor.

Orders: please contact Bookpoint Ltd, 39 Milton Park, Abingdon, Oxon OX14
4TD. Telephone: (44) 01235 400414, Fax: (44) 01235 400454. Lines are open from
9.00 – 6.00, Monday to Saturday, with a 24 hour message answering service.
Email address: orders@bookpoint.co.uk

British Library Cataloguing in Publication Data
A catalogue record for this title is available from The British Library

ISBN 0 340 782900

First published 2000
Impression number   10 9 8 7 6 5 4 3 2 1
Year   2004 2003 2002 2001 2000

Typeset by Fakenham Photosetting Limited, Fakenham, Norfolk.
Printed in Great Britain for Hodder & Stoughton Education, a division of
Hodder Headline Plc, 338 Euston Road, London NW1 3BH by Cox & Wyman
Ltd, Reading, Berkshire.

 *the Institute of Management*

The Institute of Management (IM) is the leading organisation for professional management. Its purpose is to promote the art and science of management in every sector and at every level, through research, education, training and development, and representation of members' views on management issues.

This series is commissioned by IM Enterprises Limited, a subsidiary of the Institute of Management, providing commercial services.

Management House,
Cottingham Road,
Corby,
Northants NN17 1TT
Tel: 01536 204222;
Fax: 01536 201651
Website: http://www.inst-mgt.org.uk

Registered in England no 3834492
Registered office: 2 Savoy Court, Strand,
London WC2R 0EZ

Contents

Unlock your potential   5

Get started   9

Master the monsters   18

Position yourself   32

Inspect your kit   49

Make it happen   65

Travel hopefully   80

Unlock your potential

Do you ever feel you could do more, feel more, live more and be more than you are? Most of us do. The subject of our book is *unlocking* potential – the potential you haven't yet tapped.

'A musician must make music, an artist must paint, a poet must write, if he is to be ultimately happy. What a man can be, he must be. This need ... refers to the desire for self-fulfilment, namely for the tendency in him to become actualized ... the desire to become more and more what one is, to become everything that one is capable of becoming.'

Abraham Maslow, psychologist

Our aspiration is that by working through these pages you will:

- feel more competent and comfortable within yourself
- understand and handle things that are blocking you
- become everything that you are capable of becoming.

Unlocking potential is seldom a single flash of insight. The secret, we believe, is that there *is* no secret, no magic formula. It is more of a practical journey with common-sense as companion. Everyone can make that journey.

A map of the chapters

Get started – what potential means and the keys to unlocking it

Master the monsters – the mental processes that underpin the fulfilment and blocking of potential

Position yourself – where you have been, where you are now, where you are headed

Inspect your kit – your values, intelligence, traits and capabilities

Make it happen – goals, options, plans and making it happen

Travel hopefully – ideas for making the journey more enjoyable and successful

There are two sides to potential: what you bring and what is out there. Some of the chapters are more concerned with your *personal world* – self-control, self-esteem, self-knowledge, self-handicapping and self-awareness. The others focus on the *outer world* of people, experience, actions, opportunities and constraints, successes and setbacks.

Some suggestions
- Work your way through these chapters at a relaxed pace. Take short breaks from the daily routine to read a few pages.
- Later, when you have put the book aside, you can mull over the thoughts stimulated by what you have read. Give your unconscious mind an opportunity to digest the data.
- You can do the reading and mulling on the bus or the train, but you also need quality time with pen and paper to plan your way forward.
- Use a highlighter to mark points you particularly

want to remember. And a pen to complete the exercises and to note your thoughts and reactions in the margins.

- Many people will find it helpful to discuss thoughts about their potential with a friend or a mentor. It helps to 'sort things through'.
- Take time to observe as well as think. Watch what you yourself do. Give yourself feedback. Watch what others do and learn from them.

'From the beginning, I would assess people who were successful and wonder how they got where they were. What is it about them? How do they handle this? And then I would try it on like a suit of clothes and see if it would work for me.'

Demi Moore, actress and film star

? Test Yourself

How passionately do you feel?

Robert Heller has written eloquently of the duty people have to themselves: 'the obligation to ensure that they are in the right job and employed in the right way – "right" meaning what suits your wishes and abilities, and where both can be fully realised. Life is too short to be unhappy, uncommitted or unsuccessful in your work, and there are always opportunities.'

How passionately do you feel this applies to you?

- I just do not believe it   1
- Life isn't like that   2

- Maybe   3
- I agree   4
- I feel this passionately   5

Stop now if your rating is anything less than 3. Return this book to Barnes and Noble or Waterstones, get a refund. It is not for you. If you score 3, then proceed with caution, for what you read may be hard to swallow. If you have 4 or 5, then full-steam ahead – unlock your potential! Fulfilling yourself requires an act of faith, faith in yourself and faith that you can and will do it.

Get started

This chapter:
- explores what 'potential' means
- identifies three keys to unlock it
- zeroes in on zones of fulfilment

1. Valuing yourself

So many people say they do not live up to their potential. The volume of dammed-up potential is like an enormous untapped reservoir of talent and emotion. We asked some of our friends what unlocking that potential meant, and this is what they said:

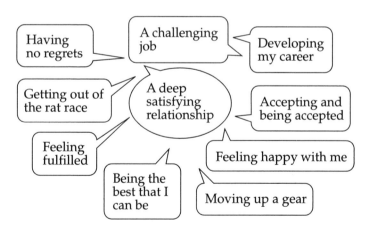

Having no regrets

A challenging job

Developing my career

Getting out of the rat race

A deep satisfying relationship

Accepting and being accepted

Feeling fulfilled

Being the best that I can be

Feeling happy with me

Moving up a gear

? Test Yourself

Complete the sentence:

'Unlocking my potential means . . .'

Whatever it might mean to you, it is unique because you are unique. But there are common threads running through everyone's wish for fulfilment:

- We deeply want to value ourselves, to feel we have intrinsic worth. Not just because of our achievements or our good looks or our jobs or the Mercedes Benz in the driveway. To use the words of Carl Rogers, a famous psychologist, we want to feel 'unconditional positive regard' for ourselves.
- Another universal aspect to fulfilment is being in tune with the world around us. We want to feel we have a part in the wider scheme of things. We want to be valued by others as well as by ourselves.
- Making informed choices is a third essential aspect: choosing what to be; choosing how to behave; choosing relationships; choosing what to develop and what to discard. Choice means that we are responsible for ourselves, which can be both exciting and scary.

In short, the keys to unlocking your potential are:

- caring deeply for yourself
- feeling connected to and in harmony with the people and events in your world
- accepting responsibility and making choices.

?

Test Yourself

The keys to your potential

How do you rate yourself? How much do you agree with these statements. Any you want to strengthen?

	Disagree			Agree	
Self love. I really value myself. I feel I am a worthwhile person.	1	2	3	4	5
In harmony. I feel part of and in harmony with the people and events in my world.	1	2	3	4	5
Personal responsibility. For better or worse it is I who control my fate. I am responsible for me.	1	2	3	4	5

2. A journey

People sometimes talk as though 'potential' is some kind of higher *state,* a place of being. Once you attain that state you have 'arrived'. You can relax, you've made it.

Instead of thinking about potential as a state, think of it as an ongoing *process.* A journey that never ends because you don't unlock your potential just once, you are unlocking it continually. Along the way you may take one step back for every two steps forward, but if you are committed and realistic then you continue to progress.

Every step forward is a realisation of your potential: cutting down the number of cigarettes today; writing a page of that novel or short story; keeping up attendance at night class; polishing the CV; working through a chapter of this book. Taken together the accumulated small steps equal a giant step forward.

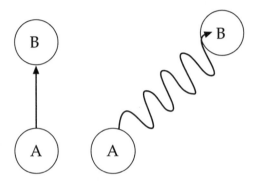

Potential as state   Potential as process

As you set out, consider where you are coming from.

? Test Yourself

Two steps forward

Think of the forward steps you have taken in the past 12 months. What were they? On the graph, make an X for each one, the greater your sense of fulfilment the higher the X. Now do the same thing in reverse for the backward steps. What does this tell you about the process of developing your potential?

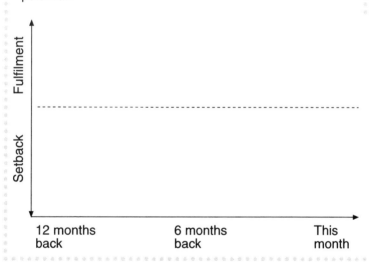

On your journey, where are you now and where do you want to be?

? Test Yourself

The personal fulfilment scale

Study these four sets of words and apply them to yourself.

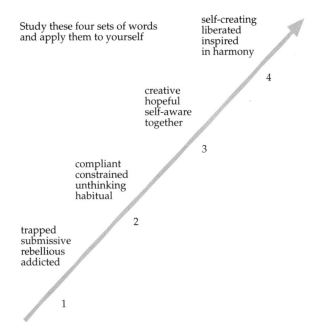

Study these four sets of words and apply them to yourself

self-creating
liberated
inspired
in harmony

4

creative
hopeful
self-aware
together

3

compliant
constrained
unthinking
habitual

2

trapped
submissive
rebellious
addicted

1

- On the 4-point scale where are you now?
- Where would you like to be in a month?
- ... in 6 months?
- ... and in 12 months?

We encourage mutual support. Give sustenance to your colleague, friend or partner along the way. Listen, give and take constructive feedback. Share this and other guide books and travel aids. However, it is a personal journey you are making. No one else can travel it. You and your history are unique so your starting-point is different. And so is your end point, because the meaning of 'success' is also uniquely yours.

Let's consider the broad direction you might want to follow.

3. How do you want to spend your time?

? **Test Yourself**
Time chart

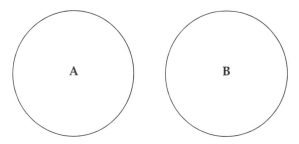

A is a pie-chart representing the sum total of your time. Think about how you use this time: (1) for yourself, such as your education or your social life, (2) to maintain and enjoy your home life and close relationships, (3) for your work. Divide the pie-chart showing what proportions of your time you would like to spend on each category. Now divide pie-chart **B** to show how your time is taken up in fact. Compare **A** and **B**. Where do they conflict? What would you change? Deciding how you would like to spend your time could be part of your goal-setting (Chapter 5).

Your ideal time chart will of course be different at different times in your life. Being at home with family will be more attractive to someone with a new house and young children than the average 19-year-old. This should give you a sense of where the opportunities for a fuller life lie.

> 'If I had my life to live over I would start barefoot earlier in the spring and I would stay that way later in the fall. I would go to more dances. I would ride more merry-go-rounds. I would pick more daisies.'
>
> Nadine Stair, 85 years old, Louisville, Kentucky

The next test zeroes in on these three zones of fulfilment.

?

Test Yourself

Fulfilment zones

Tick all of the statements with which you *strongly* identify.

1. Fulfilling myself and doing the things that please me
- I am not being stretched, my potential isn't being used to the full. ☐
- I am not doing nearly as much learning and developing as I would like. ☐
- I want to feel better about myself. My self-esteem has taken a beating. ☐
- I just feel that there is a lot more I can be doing. ☐
- I want to develop/become more involved in outside interests and activities. ☐

2. Maintaining home life and close relationships
- I want to spend a lot more time with my family or friends. ☐

- I want to develop/maintain a close relationship with someone who is special to me. □
- I want to see more of my children/grand-children growing up. □
- I want to change the pace, to get out from under the daily pressures and get a life. □
- I want to adapt my lifestyle to fit with the stage of life I am at now. □

3. Being successful and satisfied in my work and career
- I want to be sure my career is taking me where I want to go. □
- The work I am doing is not what I enjoy. I want to change that. □
- I want to be sure that the work is right for me and how I want to live my life now and in the future. □
- I want to expand myself and my horizons within the existing work. □
- I want to explore other options for someone with my interests and experience. □

Which zone has the most ticks? Is this where you want to put your energies and time? Or is there one single item that by itself carries more weight than any other?

4. The challenge

- What three points of most interest have you drawn from this chapter?
- What three questions would you like to explore in the remaining chapters?
- What do you want to get out of this book?

Master the monsters

In this chapter we turn our attention inwards to the world of the mind. We explore:
- the processing that goes on when you fulfil or fail to reach your potential
- the negative processes that drive you to fail
- how to understand and master the personal monsters that are handicapping you.

1. The inner world of potential

To unlock your full potential you need to know your inner world in some depths. Some people find that counselling in some form or another works best for them. Others learn about who they are and what makes them tick by practising introspection (i.e. looking inwards) and self-assessment. Understanding yourself allows you to play to your strengths, develop what needs developing, and manage yourself well in difficult situations.

The model on the next page describes what happens when potential is unlocked and what happens when it is blocked.

The *executive self* (A) is the centre for self-control, judgement and decision-making. It is located in the physical brain just behind your forehead. Damage it and you can be left incapable of voluntary action. This area of the brain is also central to conscious experience.

Self-esteem (B) is the inner sense of being valued. It has powerful effects on your thinking and on your actions. If you have high self-esteem you are very likely to show

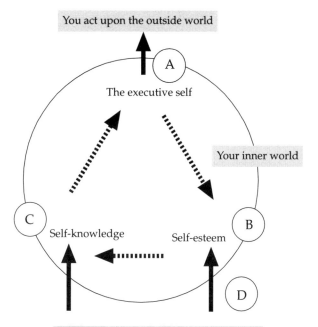

The inner world model

greater persistence and drive for success than other people. You will be more resilient, less easily depressed and less vulnerable to day-to-day setbacks.

Self-knowledge (C) is the large stock of things you know and believe about yourself, though you are conscious of only part of it at any one time. Your self-knowledge is at times blind and biased, sometimes in your favour, sometimes against. The accuracy of your self-knowledge plays a crucial part in the validity of your perceptions and the effectiveness of your judgement.

? ## Test Yourself

Assessing your inner world

On the whole, how would you assess your inner world?
Circle the numbers that best indicate your self-assessment:

	Disagree			Agree	
Executive self. I have a strong sense of responsibility, of being in control, of being able to make choices.	1	2	3	4	5
Self-esteem. In general, I feel good about myself and value who and what I am.	1	2	3	4	5
Self-knowledge. I have a realistic understanding of myself, my virtues and weaknesses, my beliefs and my biases.	1	2	3	4	5

Take a moment to consider what these ratings say. Is any
aspect of your inner self a particular strength? Are there any
that you need to strengthen if you are to realise your
potential?

These processes seem to work together something like this.
Suppose you have had a long-standing row with your
partner over some issue. You (the executive self) might
hold your resentment in check. Acting openly and
constructively, you resolve the conflict in a way that brings
you and your partner closer together. You feel pleased with
yourself, your self-esteem is enhanced (A→B). You learn to

understand yourself better and how to handle conflicts constructively (B→C). Your sense of internal control grows and you behave ever more competently in the outside world (C→A). The experience gives you confidence to consider the impression you make and the impact your actions have on others (D). This leads to quality feedback and further growth in your self-knowledge and self-esteem. In short, handling the conflict reinforces your feelings of self-worth, self-control and sense that you are in harmony with your world.

Of course, it does not always work like that. Instead, you (the executive self) might just totally lose it. In your rage you tear strips off your partner so badly that the relationship is irreparably damaged. Alternatively you might choose to 'keep the peace' but silently nurse your anger and resentment all the while. In your imagination you magnify the cause of the conflict out of all proportion. The sniping and squabbling that ensue eventually erode and destroy the relationship. The upshot is the same in either event. You are filled with negative emotions, you feel bereft, guilty and inadequate (A→B). You come to believe that no one can be trusted. Or that you are a hopeless case and cannot maintain a relationship (B→C). These beliefs block you from taking risks with new relationships (C→A) and from seeking feedback (D).

Does this remind you of any personal incident? If you had a chance to replay that incident, what would you do the same? What would you do differently?

Your behaviour in the first example is potential-enhancing. In the second it is potential-blocking.

We will now examine each process in some detail. But remember, they operate together – everything affects everything.

2. The executive self

When you feel able to make choices – to take or not to take an action – that is the executive self operating. You feel responsible for yourself and your behaviour. The desire to have control is one of the strongest motives in people, hence the despair of those who lose their liberty.

Restricted control and choice may lead to anxiety and cause aggression against those in power. It happens with pupils and teachers, staff and bosses, and foot soldiers and officers. But it happens most of all with children and parents. Unlocking potential may involve some sorting out of the feelings from those relationships.

This newspaper report recently appeared. A teacher took his own life the day before a visit from the school inspector. The note he left contained the words: "I did my best but my best wasn't good enough." He was, said a saddened colleague, a fine teacher, highly respected but a perfectionist.

When did this poor man become a perfectionist? When he was awarded his teaching certificate? When he became head of department? You can bet the roots go back to his very earliest days – when he was reminded constantly of the high standards he had to meet. Because his best was probably not good enough as a child, it would never be good enough.

Perfectionists tend to have impossibly high standards. Janet is a DIY enthusiast and a perfectionist. She meticulously wallpapers the insides of closets no one could possibly see. Henry is an R & D chemist who keeps on testing new drugs far, far beyond the standard required. Because of his perfectionism he fails to meet a crucial delivery deadline. Result: an expensive research programme down the drain.

The Janets and Henrys of the world do not choose to be that way. Each has a strong 'Be Perfect driver' which is not of their choosing. It does not come from the executive self. It is compulsive and it prevents them from choosing standards that are appropriate to the circumstance.

This happens to many people. They are exposed from early days to messages from parents or guardians repeated thousands of times. These become lodged in the mind inevitably and indelibly. So, even when the parents are long gone, their instructions keep coming through clearly. 'Be good'. 'Keep things in the family'. 'Be kind and helpful to others'. 'Big boys don't cry.' 'Good girls keep themselves pure'. Can you hear one of those messages in your mind?

Here are some of the common drivers that handicap people.

Driver	The meaning and consequences
Be Perfect	Having impossibly high standards – never satisfied with what you do, you exceed what is practical
Please Others	Always doing what others ask – not what *you* want
Hurry Up	Always rushing about – 'busy fool', leaving things until too late
Try harder	Striving, what counts is the effort not the result – lack of focus, persevering too far
Be Strong	Shouldering the burdens without complaint – so no one helps you

? Test Yourself

Assessing your drivers

With an X mark yourself on each driver, the higher the X the stronger the driver. Up to a point they pose no serious problem; beyond that they are real handicaps.

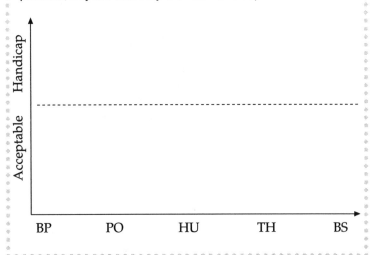

For each of these compulsive drivers there is an antidote –
an *allower* that puts the executive self back in charge and the
compulsion back in its box. If you find one that is right for
you, repeat it to yourself before falling asleep and when
you waken up. Write it on a card and put it where you can
see it.

Driver	*Allower*	
Be Perfect	You're good enough as you are	☐
Please Others	Please yourself	☐
Hurry Up	Take your time	☐
Try Harder	Do it, get it finished	☐
Be Strong	Be open and express your wants	☐

Another expression for the executive self is *locus of control.*
Having an internal *locus of control* is an asset. 'Internal'
means *you* exercising choice, *you* being in control of your
fate. As our model of the inner world showed, an internal
locus develops out of the decisions and actions you take in
the outer world. Being assertive about what you believe and
want is an expression and a reinforcer of your internal
locus.

What follows is not a psychometric test but it does give a
broad indication of where you see your locus of control.

?

Test Yourself

Locus of control

Circle the number to show how strongly you agree/disagree with each statement. Numbers on the left always mean 'disagree', and those on the right always mean 'agree'.

	Disagree				Agree
Getting ahead is about what you can do, not who you know	1	2	3	4	5
I am too old to change	5	4	3	2	1
If someone hates me there's not a lot I can do about it	5	4	3	2	1
Most people can learn to be leaders – it's not a matter of birth	1	2	3	4	5
A good way to handle a problem is not to think about it	5	4	3	2	1
Promotions are earned through hard work and persistence	1	2	3	4	5
I am very persevering – and I usually accomplish what I set out to do	1	2	3	4	5
Because no one can predict the future there's little point in making plans	5	4	3	2	1
I won't make resolutions because I don't usually keep them	5	4	3	2	1
I believe we are masters of our own fates	1	2	3	4	5
Total score					

Interpreting your scores

If your total score is 40 or higher you probably feel in control of your life and what happens to you, the good and the bad. You are likely to take initiative in relationships, work and career. A score of 30 to 39 also suggests an internal locus of control, though less definitely.

If you scored 10 or lower the opposite is probably true – you feel you don't have much control over what happens. A score of 11 to 19 carries a similar, though less pronounced meaning. In order to strengthen your executive self you may need to take more risks in the outside world. Not stupid risks, or ill-informed risks, but risks nonetheless. The more practice you have the better and easier it becomes.

A score in the 20–29 falls in between. There is real scope for you to develop your internal locus of control further.

3. Self-esteem

'Self-esteem is how you feel when you are striving wholeheartedly for worthwhile things; it's how you experience yourself when you are using your abilities to the fullest in the service of what you deeply value. It's not about displaying your traits advantageously or showing that yours are better than someone else's … what feeds your self-esteem – meeting challenges with high effort and using your abilities to help others – is also what makes for a productive and constructive life.'

Professor Carol Dweck, psychologist

'Transactional analysis' (TA) was developed to help individuals in psychotherapy. It is now applied quite extensively to developing individuals and organisations. It gives us insight into self-esteem. Remember: self-esteem grows when we act competently in our relationships and behaviour. Self-esteem (and its absence) is also the product of accumulated judgements about being good or bad, worthwhile or worthless. These judgements ('strokes') come from other people as well as from within oneself.

The TA principles provide a solid platform for building positive self-esteem:

- Everyone deserves worth and dignity ('people are OK'). That doesn't mean I will respect everything you do or that I won't conflict with you. But as a starting point I respect you as a human being. I expect you to consider me and others in the same light.
- Regardless of differences in background and accomplishments, you and I are the equal of one another as human beings.
- We each have the capacity to think and decide. We have personal responsibility for deciding what we want from life. No one else has responsibility for or controls my fate or yours.

Take a few minutes to mull over each of these principles. How deeply do you believe/disbelieve them? Can you think of recent experiences when you have lived up or down to the principle? How did you feel? Can you remember anyone telling you 'You're OK?' How did that make you feel?

Our self-esteem may vary from day to day, depending on the inflow of positive and negative strokes. But our unique personal history endows us with a more or less consistent level of self-esteem.

? Test Yourself

Sources of self-esteem and their effects

Here is what can happen when you feel valued or devalued by yourself or significant others. Each quadrant shows a range of typical reactions.

Other people's views of me	**My views of myself**	
	I'm OK	I'm not OK
You are OK	*Healthy self-esteem –* confident, get-on-with-it, behave constructively	*Low self-esteem –* please others, feel inferior, discount compliments
You're not OK	*Struggling self-esteem –* feel rejected, self-defensive, rebellious	*Very low self-esteem –* put things off, feel hopeless, alienated

- In the average week, what percentage of your time do you spend in each quadrant?
- Is there anything you want to change in any quadrant?
- What options can you think of to bring about the change?

'No one can make you feel inferior without your consent.'

Eleanor Roosevelt

4. Self-knowledge

'Recognizing strengths and compensating for weaknesses represent the first step in achieving positive self-regard ... The second element ... is to keep working on and developing one's talents.'

Bennis and Nanus

We will dig deeper into your strengths in Chapter 4. For the moment consider how you can boost all aspects of your inner self – your executive self, your self-esteem and your self-knowledge:

DON'T

- make excuses or keep telling yourself you are not up to it.
- duck out of learning new things to spare yourself discomfort.
- limit yourself to challenges that are within your comfort stretch.
- avoid risks.
- see failure as a cause for shame or as confirming your inferiority.
- put yourself down – 'I'm not very good at ...'
- deny positive things as if they do not count.
- blame the system.

Is there anything in this list of Don'ts you will stop doing, starting now? Is there anything in the list below that you will start doing now, or do more of?

DO

- be honest, face facts – don't delude yourself.
- be open to new learning – be prepared to feel anxious or incompetent.
- develop and apply your learning skills and habits of learning.
- take on challenges that are stretching, doing it with enthusiasm.
- persevere and work hard to master those challenges.
- risk failures and learn from them.
- think strategically – 'how can I do it better or differently next time?'
- be forgiving of yourself and others.
- keep on practising.

5. The challenge

- What three points are you going to remember from this chapter?
- Which ones are you going to put into action?
- When exactly will you do that?
- What can happen to prevent you doing that?
- What are you going to do to make sure that doesn't happen?

Position yourself

The journey so far has taken you into the inner reaches of yourself. Few people seek fulfilment in this inner world of the spirit, fewer turn their backs on the outside world to embrace the contemplative life. That is not the way for most of us. Our growth and fulfilment are bound up with the world of people, partners, family, trains, business, public service, shopping and entertainment.

This chapter looks outward at the world and your place in it – past, present, and future. In it we invite you to:

- look back and take stock of the past
- review important aspects and areas of your present life, and
- look forward to where you would like to be.

What constraints and opportunities have you encountered along the way? What traces has the past left? What are the filters through which you now see the world? In what areas is your potential most likely to unfold? What are the important roles in your life? And how will your life be in the future?

We offer a framework of nine areas to help you shape your recollections and reflections. All are universally relevant but not equally and not always. In relating them to your life the important questions for you are:

- are you doing yourself justice in the areas relevant to you?
- are you laying the foundation for success in each one?
- are you striking an optimum balance?

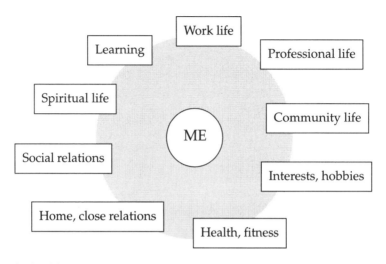

The key life areas

We will explore the nine areas from the three perspectives – where you have come from, where you are now, and where you want to be.

1. Looking back

If you do not have a sense of your past, how can you make sense of the present?

?

Test Yourself

Your life journey

Everyone can remember defining moments in their lives – critical incidents, significant people, proud achievements, major setbacks. Some were high points, some were low points. On the next page is a time line with your birth at the bottom and today at the top. Plot the progress of your life by marking the critical highs and lows with an X. Join up the Xs to get the overall picture.

Low		You today, now		*High*
points				*points*

Low	You at birth	*High*
points		*points*

When you have drawn your lifeline use it to think about the significant turning points in your life.

- What gave/gives you the most pride? Don't skip this question!
- Where did you grasp opportunities and go with them?
- Are there any major lows which led to later highs, because of choices/actions you took?
- Are there any recurring themes or patterns?

The relationship you have with the world around is like that of a river to the riverbank. In finding its way to the sea, the river sometimes pushes easily through the land. Sometimes the riverbanks will be too rocky and mountains will block the way. Then the river must find a new way round or cut a new channel through the rock before it can reach the sea. Or it gives up, loses direction, and divides itself into minor streams going nowhere in particular.

Finding a match between your aspirations and the opportunities the world presents is sometimes straightforward and clear. At other times the challenges and constraints mean you must take another route, cut a new path or find a different way to satisfy your desire for growth and fulfilment. Or, like the diverted river, you accept the constraints, make excuses, and occupy yourself with inconsequential activities.

Thinking back to the lifeline you plotted, can you think of defining moments when:

- Bingo! The opportunities matched your aspirations?
- You had to find a different way because the path was blocked?

- You gave up in the face of the obstacles and constraints?

The object of looking backward is enlightenment not self-blame. If you can identify what worked for you in the past, you can do more of the same in the future. And, conversely, you can learn so much from failure. If you cannot recall any failures it means you haven't been stretching yourself sufficiently.

- So what can you learn from these moments in your history?
- What can you do more of?
- What can you do less of?
- What might you do differently?

People may give up because they impose constraints on themselves. 'I'm only a housewife', 'People like me don't become merchant bankers, go to university, start up their own business'. They accept at face value restrictions of class, or gender or age. Or they fall into the trap of pigeonholing themselves – and other people. These obstacles are from within, not outside.

Ellen Langer, an American psychologist, describes this kind of thinking as 'mindlessness'. You become 'trapped by categories' – masculine-feminine, success-failure, old-young – which you have created to make a coherent picture of the world and yourself. You rely on stereotypical thinking to decide what you *cannot* do.

Betty challenged those stereotypes. An active and busy 75-year-old, she visited her GP about her 'bad leg'. The

GP, not knowing Betty very well, suggested that she shouldn't be too surprised that her leg was troubling her. After all she was 'getting on a bit in years'. Betty's robust reply was that her other leg was the same age as the one that was troubling her – and it was doing just fine.

You can also get trapped by the familiar – lulled into a mental laziness which prevents you really paying attention to your world. At the simplest level this is used in word trap riddles.

Q. What do you call a tree that grows from acorns?
A. Oak
Q. What do you call a funny story?
A. Joke
Q. What do you call the sound made by a frog?
A. Croak
Q. What do you call the white of an egg?
A. Yolk.*

These mindsets can close you off from new information. They handicap your ability to think outside the box when facing the challenges and opportunities of a changing environment. Thinking outside the box is important for companies as much as for individuals. Revlon's marketing strategy changed dramatically for the better when they realised that the company doesn't sell make-up: it sells hope.

Are there any straitjackets from the past you still carry around? Think hard. Ask your closest friends. To unlock your potential, rid yourself of any blinkers that constrict your thinking and block your initiative.

* To spare you frustration, yolk is not the white of an egg. We didn't get it first time either.

Continuing to reflect on your past, consider again the key life areas.

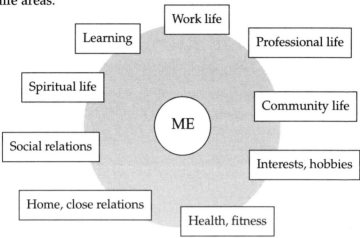

Test Yourself

Over the past 5 years or so:

- were you able to strike a good balance?
- in which area did you develop the greatest confidence?
- what memories do you want to keep alive?
- did you lay the groundwork for future fulfilment?

2. Your life in the present

Now step out of the past into the present. Your daily life is spent playing a number of roles. Partner, child, parent, learner, teacher, friend, citizen, employee, entrepreneur, owner, supplier, consumer. The mix and pattern change over time. Any one role can take up a significant amount of your time and mental-emotional energy. Sometimes the roles will connect and enhance one another, at other times they won't. And sometimes they will be in conflict with one other.

Work life

Learning

Professional life

Spiritual life

Community life

Health, fitness

Interests, hobbies

Social relations

Home, close
relations

?

Test Yourself

Your roles, how do they fit?

- Make a list of your six most relevant roles.
- Estimate the hours you gave to each role in the past seven days.
- Is this typical?
- How much time do you really want to give?
- What's getting in the way?
- What can you do to change this?

Your key roles	Hours spent:	
	Actual	Desired
1.		
2.		
3.		
4.		
5.		
6.		

In a life and career development workshop, Jeremy identified parenting as a high priority. Yet on reviewing his week he was shocked to find he gave it just 30 minutes a day. And most of that in telling his sons to hurry up, stop fighting, turn down the TV, and give him some peace.

Carry's approach was different. She always sat down with her partner to talk about the week ahead. They wanted to ensure they had quality time for each other and for their separate priorities. This worked. Carry found the time for the relationship, to study for a part time degree and to fit in a regular visit to the gym.

One of the great difficulties today is finding time for self-development. And it is universal.

Maria, who works for one of the international accounting giants in Bulgaria, writes: 'I have been awfully busy ... I have been working without a break for six weeks, which is really crazy. This weekend I felt I had to take a rest otherwise I would get ill ... but I passed the last ACCA exams ... it was a great effort but I did it!'

Part of the secret is to set priorities. Part is to recognise the pressure that comes from your internal drivers and to curb them (Chapter 2). Part is integrating your learning with your current activities – to learn from what you would be doing anyway. And, when you have options, choosing activities and projects that expand your learning. When you coach children in football or swimming you are developing skills that are transferable to work. So too when you work as a volunteer for Childline, Age Concern or other voluntary organisations. We, the authors, use our roles as writers, consultants and researchers to develop skills and know-how we want to develop.

> Can you see opportunities, new or existing, that would enable you to learn and develop your potential?

There is a temptation to think: 'Somewhere out there is the perfect opportunity. Once I discover it there will be no holding me back.' Underlying this thinking is the implicit faith that 'I have what it takes'. Regular stories in the press about overnight e-commerce millionaires stoke the belief.

Realising your potential is more than finding the right opportunity, of course. It is about nurturing and growing burgeoning capabilities which requires a great deal of hard application. The maxim of twenty percent inspiration and eighty percent perspiration applies in full.

> 'It's amazing how the harder I work and the more I practice, the luckier I get.'
> Gary Player, championship golfer

'Lifelong learning' has become the grail of this twenty first century. The flexibility it embodies is quite a modern thing. Traditionally, people 'knew their place' and the 'right way to behave' at appropriate stages in life. In 'As You Like It ' Shakespeare described the seven ages of man. People implicitly accepted a set programme of ages and stages: being silent and not heard as a child, then stormy adolescence, followed by settling down into a job and marriage, becoming parents and grandparents, and finally retiring. People were expected to 'act their age'. To be out of sync with this implicit social timetable made people feel uncomfortable and odd-man-out.

In today's world people are more liberated. They have many fewer age-bound expectations. There are many 25-year-olds who aren't ready to settle down. And 45-year-olds who want to experience new careers and new styles of living. And there are plenty of 65-year-olds studying for degrees and acting out life-long ambitions to travel round the world. The mottoes for living fully in today's world are: 'use it or lose it' and 'try it, you'll like it'.

> 'Optimal matches between individuals and their environments are only possible if there are opportunities for people to change direction in mid-life and perhaps later too.'
> Daniel Levinson and colleagues, researchers and writers

Levinson describes adulthood as a series of alternating stable and transitional periods. In early adulthood we formulate our dream – our preferred way of life. This includes what we want to work at, our relationships and how we spend our leisure time. During the stable periods we know what life structure we're trying to build. The transition periods are about reviewing and questioning – and perhaps refining the dream.

? # Test Yourself

Refining the dream.

How does your life dream look from where you are standing?
- *Health, fitness.* Are you as healthy and active as you want to be?
- *Home, close relations.* How much time and energy do you give to your family roles?
- *Social relationships.* Are you giving enough time to maintaining your social networks?
- *Spiritual life.* What are some of the causes you believe in and support? What belief systems?
- *Learning.* What active learning are you involved in?
- *Work life.* What words best describe your feelings about your work?
- *Professional life.* How important is your professional identity? What standards are important to you?
- *Community life.* How involved are you in your local community?
- *Interests, hobbies.* What do you do for fun?

3. You in the future

Now on to your future. Think for a minute about how the world is changing.

Longevity
People are living longer. You can expect many years of active and healthy life after your 'retirement' from work and major family responsibilities. Your grandparents may have had only a few years to enjoy retirement. You are likely to have 20 years or more.

Multi-cultural diversity
The world is getting smaller. Trade and travel abroad are

commonplace. Life in an increasingly multi-cultural society has introduced different cultural practices and widened views of what is possible.

Learning for life
The internet gives access to an unimagined wealth of information. Gaining information is only the first step: applying it in practice is next. People now need to 'learn a living' as much as earn a living.

Jobs are temporary
Unlike earlier generations, few can expect to enjoy a steady career progression through the ranks of a single organisation. The world of work is one of continuous restructuring. Euphemisms abound for job loss – right-sizing, down-sizing, surplus to requirement, gardening leave and outplacement. New kinds of jobs are being created all the time.

Uncertainty and the pace of change
The world is in a state of flux and constant change. The future is much less predictable than it ever was. And the rate of change keeps accelerating.

? # Test Yourself

Are you ready for the future?

	Disagree				Agree
I know how I am going to add life to my years rather than just years to my life	1	2	3	4	5
I am making the most of living in a multi-cultural society	1	2	3	4	5
I am 'learning my living' – I am committed to lifelong learning	1	2	3	4	5
I don't expect a job for life and I have made my plans for this	1	2	3	4	5
I can flex, adapt and handle change reasonably well	1	2	3	4	5

Without computers your way of life would not be possible – something everyone takes for granted until the next Millennium Bug scare. Many people now work in jobs not even thought of ten years ago. What next after cloned sheep, cloned body parts, limb transplants, emails by telephone and the human genome project? The mind boggles.

? Test Yourself

Blue sky thinking

What hopes do you have? What possibilities can you see for yourself in the future? Be creative – think laterally. What do you fear? What challenges are likely? Where will they come from?

	Hopes, opportunities	Fears, challenges
health and fitness		
home and family		
relationships		
spiritual life		
learning		
work life		
professional life		
community life		
interests and hobbies		

- What information do you need to confirm whether you are on the right track?
- How can you best mobilise your strengths and resources to bring your hopes to life?
- What can you do to prepare for the challenges and to conquer the fears?
- What can you do to ensure your obstacles and gaps don't get in the way?

Here is a creative way of exploring how you would like the rest of your life to be. It can help you rethink where you want to put your time and energy. Imagine: it is many years into the future and you have passed on to higher things. Your obituary appears in *The Times*.

? **Test Yourself**

Your newspaper obituary

- How would the writer summarise your life?
- What would your epitaph say? Be honest.
- What would you like it to say?
- What can you do now to make it read as you'd like it to?
- What does this tell you about the kind of future you want – and what you need to do NOW to make that future happen?

'To laugh often and much; to win the respect of intelligent people and the affection of children; to earn the appreciation of honest critics and endure the betrayal of false friends; to appreciate beauty, and to find the best in others; to leave the world a bit better, whether by a healthy child, a garden patch, or a redeemed social condition; to know even one life has breathed easier because you lived. This is to have succeeded.'

Ralph Waldo Emerson, American writer

The challenge

- Name three things you have learned about yourself from your review of the past.
- What three questions will help you formulate your dream for the future?

Inspect your kit

The purpose of the chapter is to continue discarding the beliefs that handicap your potential. And to audit the strengths you take with you on the journey:

- your values
- your special brand of intelligence
- your personality
- your capabilities

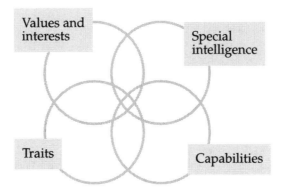

You are more than the sum of these parts of course. There is an inner core we call 'heart' or 'spirit' that brings the rest to life. It inspires us to grow and perfect ourselves.

Completing the chapter will take time. Take two runs at the self-assessments – the first to get your initial thoughts down, and the second to assess yourself more deliberately. If you would like a more complete assessment of yourself, a qualified chartered psychologist will be able to help.

? Test Yourself

Accentuate the positive
- List three things you have achieved that give you pride.
- What does each achievement say about you?
- What hidden dream do you have about the future? Do you have the potential to make it real?

1. Your values and interests

Values are important – not just for individuals but for groups and organisations too. Being very clear about what you value on your personal journey will guide you when the going gets rough or uncertain.

? Test Yourself

Your values and interests
Add anything important that is missing from this list. Tick up to eight items that matter most to you. If you could have only four things from the list, which would they be? Give these double ticks. Now examine them closely, first the four then the eight. Make sure you have them firmly imprinted in your memory. Give these a central place in your vision and goals (Chapter 5).

1 **Competence:** Feeling capable and effective, being able to master the tasks I set or am set. ☐
2. **Autonomy**: Having control. Being able to make independent choices and decisions. ☐
3. **Self-esteem**: Feeling good about myself. Self-respect. ☐

4. **Personal growth**: Learning and developing my skills, knowledge, ability, and personal qualities. ☐

5. **Serving a cause:** Committing myself to a special cause and contributing to/achieving something of real value. ☐

6. **Recognition**: Being recognised and appreciated for myself or for my work. ☐

7. **Results**: Making a difference, having an impact, surmounting difficulties and getting results. ☐

8. **Balance:** Having all the important aspects of my life in harmony with sufficient time to devote to each part. ☐

9. **Family and kinship**: The satisfactions of being a spouse or parent and the deep relationships I have with my family. ☐

10. **People**: My friends and associates, enjoying their company and relationships. ☐

11. **Continuity and security**: Having a job which has a safe and predictable future. Stability and continuity. ☐

12. **Entrepreneuring**: Taking personal risk to create something new through my own efforts. ☐

13. **Innovation and change**: Seeing new possibilities and ideas, bringing them to life. Influencing change. ☐

14. **Advancement and promotion**: Rising to positions of higher stature. ☐

15. **Prosperity**: Having a good income and the lifestyle that money can buy. ☐

16. Power: Being able to direct and control people and other resources. Being in a position of power. □

17. Guiding others: Making things happen by guiding, inspiring, influencing and developing others. □

18. Being active: Doing things, making things happen, being energetic and physical. □

19. Being creative: Using my imagination, being able to express my feelings and ideas. □

20. Being expert: Being valued for my special expertise. □

Self-esteem comes from having or being what you value. And from having a job and a lifestyle that are in tune with your values and interests.

'No one should be neutral or indifferent to his work or his workplace. It is very important for a person to have a careful look at the kind of work he does. He should try to establish whether the work he does and his workplace is actually expressive of his identity, dignity and giftedness. If not, difficult choices may need to be made. If you sell your soul you ultimately buy a life of misery.'

John O'Donohue, poet and scholar

? ## Test Yourself

Which of these statements best describes the fit between your life and your values?

My work, relationships and life are pretty
much in harmony with my identity and values. ☐

I am able to fulfill some of myself and my
values but not others. It's a mixed bag, really. ☐

My work, relationships and life are very
much out of tune with who I am and my values. ☐

- Which particular core values and interests are being fulfilled?
- Which ones are not being fulfilled to your satisfaction?
- What types of work and lifestyle do you think would be most compatible with your values and identity?

Carry is 35 and married with no children. Her top values are for power, advancement and promotion, innovation and change. Jeremy is 48, also married, still has a young family to educate. He values balance, competence and continuity–security. The company they work for is going through vast amounts of change. It is disposing of production plants to concentrate on distribution and selling and creating a major call centre. Structure and job roles and new business processes have not been decided. Rumours are rife and many people feel insecure and anxious. Carry finds the current situation highly stimulating, but that is clearly not the case for Jeremy.

2. Your special intelligence

One of the strongest beliefs in popular mythology concerns IQ. Those who pass the 11-plus, obtain A levels (or, in Scotland, Highers), or get a 2:1 degree are winners. Everyone else is a loser. This is so patently untrue. There is a low correlation between IQ scores and life success. Many pre-eminent politicians and captains of industry never attended university. What is true is that you need a certain modicum of intellectual ability to process information, conceptualise, reason and analyse problems. After that other qualities make a bigger difference.

Mike is from a working-class background. His memories of his school days in Liverpool are bitter. An undiagnosed dyslexic, he was put on the scrapheap as a no-hoper by the headmaster. Today he has BSc and MSc degrees. He is a senior manager running a large training department. In the industrial sector where he works, he is an expert adviser to eastern European powers.

There are two further points about intelligence we want to make. First, there are almost certainly several kinds of intelligence, not one. Second, what you *believe* about your intelligence has enormous implications for your potential.

Multiple intelligences

Howard Gardner, an educational psychologist, has identified seven kinds. All involve the ability to reason and to solve real problems though in different spheres. Here they are, together with our examples of geniuses in each sphere.

Intelligence	Genius	You
Linguistic	Shakespeare, Noam Chomsky	☐
Musical	Beethoven, Paul McCartney	☐
Logical–mathematical	Pythagoras, Albert Einstein	☐
Spatial	Picasso, Henry Moore	☐
Bodily–kinesthetic	Nadia Commenici (gymnast), Wayne Gretzky (hockey)	☐
Intrapersonal	Pope John Paul XXXIII, Robert Burns	☐
Interpersonal	Senator George Mitchell, Oprah Winfrey	☐

Think carefully: with which form of genius do you identify most closely?

People with high *interpersonal* intelligence have deep understanding of others – what motivates them, how they work, and how to work with them. They are often successful in sales, politics, teaching, counselling, and religious occupations. Those with high *intrapersonal* intelligence have a similar ability turned inwards. They know themselves inside out. They are able to form a truthful picture of themselves and to use that picture to operate effectively in life. The 'personal' intelligences are illustrated in this case.

Jonathan, a marketing director, is small and introverted. He has a first class degree from Cambridge and an MBA. David, the sales director, is large, dominant and self-confident. He has a diploma in agriculture, no A-levels, and struggles to understand a balance sheet. Yet it was David who was nominated to succeed the managing director. Knowing himself well, he is able to play to his strengths. He has a gift for communicating in ways that make people feel special. And he can hold his own with the strong men on the Group management committee. Jonathan is self-engrossed, a chronic worrier, awkward in relationships and lacking in insight into himself and his weaknesses.

What you believe makes a difference

Regardless of how intelligent you are, your *beliefs* about intelligence have an enormous impact on your effectiveness.

? **Test Yourself**

Your theory of intelligence

1. Complete this equation by filling in the blank percentages:
   Intelligence =   % effort +   % ability

2. Which first-year undergraduates should be admitted into an honours programme?

   a) Students with very high IQ scores who don't work very hard and earn low course grades
   b) Students with average IQ scores who work very hard and earn good course grades

People tend to hold one or other of the following two theories.

Fixed theory

Intelligence is a fixed, concrete entity – you only have a certain amount. Believers in this theory give a much higher weight to ability than effort in the above equation. They also favour the a) students.

Flexible theory
Intelligence is a malleable quality which can be developed and improved through your efforts. These believers give a much higher emphasis to effort and favour the b) students.

The research of Professor Carol Dweck and others has shown consistent differences between fixed and flexible 'theorists' – children as well as adults. These differences all involve the fulfilment of potential:

Fixed theorists
• Interested in showing what they can do, proving they are intelligent
• Unwilling to expose their ignorance, more likely to shun learning opportunities
• Anxious about challenges
• See failure as a reflection of their intelligence
• Which often leads to disorganised, defensive, and helpless behaviour
• Making them more prone to depression.

Flexible theorists
• Oriented towards learning new skills
• Willing to expose their deficiencies in order to learn and improve
• Keen to undertake remedial action
• Stimulated by challenges
• See setbacks as a normal part of learning and mastery
• Setbacks are not really failures, but cues for renewed effort and new strategies.

The single most powerful lesson from this remarkable research is: these beliefs are not cast in stone, you can change them. So if you are a fixed theorist, change it now and find how good it feels!

3. Your traits

Personality traits are dispositions to behave in stable, predictable ways. Some of these ways can be potential-enhancing and some potential-defeating. For example, if you are conscientious and hard-working you will likely make the most of opportunities. But if you avoid taking risks, opportunities will pass you by.

Your traits also influence how you present yourself in the public eye. Extraverts are highly noticeable and give an impression of competence because they like to take charge. Introverts, because they shun the limelight, have less impact. And, because they say relatively little, introverts create a misleading impression of being arrogant, or shy, or switched off. Extraverts therefore will get more than their share of opportunities to shine.

Knowing your traits and how you project is clearly an advantage.

> 'Sex appeal is 50 percent what you've got and 50 percent what people think you've got.'
>
> Sophia Loren

?

Test Yourself

Your personality traits

These descriptions are similar to the items in well-established personality questionnaires. Rating yourself on them will give you a sense of your traits.

Extraverted ☐ ☐ ☐ ☐ ☐ *Introverted*
• start conversations easily   • think before I speak
• enjoy being part of a group   • enjoy my privacy
• take charge of things   • keep in the background

Agreeable ☐ ☐ ☐ ☐ ☐ *Tough-minded*
• seldom take offense   • look for hidden motives
• take an interest in others   • tend to hold a grudge
• seen as a bit of a soft touch   • quick to pass judgement

Worrying ☐ ☐ ☐ ☐ ☐ *Confident*
• often feel blue   • relaxed most of the time
• think about past mistakes   • comfortable with myself
• afraid I will do the wrong thing   • not easily discouraged

Conventional ☐ ☐ ☐ ☐ ☐ *Wide-ranging*
• prefer tried and tested ways   • look for new ways & ideas
• 'if it works don't change it'   • read challenging material
• dislike theoretical discussion   • prefer variety to routine

Conscientious ☐ ☐ ☐ ☐ ☐ *Free spirit*
• do things right   • break the rules
• do things by the book   • leave things lying around
• self-disciplined and orderly   • put off unpleasant tasks

- For each of your five traits, write down a practical advantage and a disadvantage you have experienced.
- Now, write how you can make the most of the advantages in the future
- . . . and how you can minimise the disadvantages.

Personality is similar to intelligence in this sense. If you see it as fixed, then it becomes a handicap. If you see it as mouldable, and you work at it, then it becomes an asset. Neither your behaviour nor your fate is predetermined. Certainly you will always retain the dispositions received at birth. But there is great scope for self-insight and for developing the skills that will make the most of your endowment.

4. Your capabilities

?

Test Yourself

Your abilities

Your tasks here are to identify:
- 👍 your top 10 capabilities– we want you to boast!
- 👂 capabilities you may want to discuss with a mentor or friend
- ⍦ the 6 capabilities you would most like to develop or strengthen

Bring this analysis forward when you come to the next chapter.

A. Managing yourself	👍	👂	⍦
1. *Know yourself* – understand yourself, your strengths and development needs	☐	☐	☐
2. *Esteem yourself* – like yourself	☐	☐	☐
3. *Control yourself* – control yourself under pressure, crisis or provocation	☐	☐	☐
4. *Do the right thing* – be true and honest in your actions	☐	☐	☐

5. *Give hope* – see things from a constructive and optimistic perspective   ☐ ☐ ☐

6. *Make an impact* – project a positive image through your grooming, manner and voice   ☐ ☐ ☐

B. Adapting   👍 👂 📡

1. *Initiate* – originate action without needing direction from others   ☐ ☐ ☐

2. *Persevere* – stick to a task, act persistently on a goal   ☐ ☐ ☐

3. *Spring back* – adapt positively and constructively to setbacks   ☐ ☐ ☐

4. *Tolerate ambiguity* – maintain balance and performance despite uncertainty and confusion   ☐ ☐ ☐

5. *Structure* – bring order and purpose to muddled thinking and situations   ☐ ☐ ☐

6. *Control* – ensure plans are followed up and objectives met   ☐ ☐ ☐

7. *Feel* – appreciate and respond to your own and others' needs and feelings   ☐ ☐ ☐

C. Thinking   👍 👂 📡

1. *Open your mind* – to people, ideas, possibilities and learning   ☐ ☐ ☐

2. *Think objectively* – consider and weigh all the relevant facts and alternatives before committing yourself   ☐ ☐ ☐

3. *Strike a balance*– between your feelings and reason before you decide or act   ☐ ☐ ☐

4. *Make decisions* – weigh information, consider the consequences, then make and stand by the decisions ☐ ☐ ☐
5. *Think critically* – analyse events into essential parts and deduce underlying causes and effects ☐ ☐ ☐
6. *Attend to details* – be precise and accurate when it counts ☐ ☐ ☐
7. *Develop new concepts* – to grasp situations and draw sound conclusions ☐ ☐ ☐
8. *See the 'big picture'* – take a wide perspective, observe events, note links and relationships ☐ ☐ ☐
9. *Reason with words* – comprehend and reason quickly and accurately with words and verbal arguments ☐ ☐ ☐
10. *Reason with numbers* – comprehend and reason quickly and accurately with numerical data and ideas ☐ ☐ ☐

D. Communicating

1. *Listen attentively* – fully understand the meaning and feeling behind the words ☐ ☐ ☐
2. *Express yourself* – openly and fully even at the risk of being unpopular ☐ ☐ ☐
3. *Speak convincingly* – get your ideas and arguments across, make an impression ☐ ☐ ☐
4. *Write convincingly* – get your ideas and arguments across,

make an impression ☐ ☐ ☐
5. *Speak in public* – plan and deliver
presentations, get your ideas
and arguments across ☐ ☐ ☐
6. *Select the right mode* – of
communication to suit situation,
purpose and audience ☐ ☐ ☐

E. Relating 👍 👂 📡

1. *Understand people* – and
respond appropriately and
sensitively to them ☐ ☐ ☐
2. *Influence* – lead others willingly
towards the goal or action you
have set ☐ ☐ ☐
3. *Relate* – manage interactions
and relationships with diverse
kinds of people ☐ ☐ ☐
4. *Help* – give support and advice,
help others to succeed ☐ ☐ ☐
5. *Facilitate* – get the best out of
a group by enabling them to
work together effectively ☐ ☐ ☐
6. *Manage meetings* – prepare,
manage or chair meetings ☐ ☐ ☐
7. *Contribute* – contribute
effectively to the task and
human relations of a team ☐ ☐ ☐
8. *Network* – develop and maintain
helpful contacts with a range of
people ☐ ☐ ☐
9. *Manage up* – maintain co-
operative relations with people
of influence ☐ ☐ ☐

F. Applying your experience   👍   👂   📶

1. *Sector experience* – experience
    of a particular industry, public
    service, education or voluntary
    sector   ☐   ☐   ☐
2. *Specialist experience* – from
    working in a discipline or
    subject area, or with a product
    or service   ☐   ☐   ☐
3. *Computing experience* – with
    software, PCs, networks,
    e-commerce, mainframes etc   ☐   ☐   ☐
4. *Cultural experience* –
    understand a culture or
    subculture   ☐   ☐   ☐

The challenge

- What three interesting thoughts will you take forward
  from this chapter?
- What is the single thing that you value most in
  yourself?
- What insights about your strengths and weaknesses
  will you include in any plans for the future?
- Can you think of any other way you can benefit from
  your self-analysis?

Make it happen

You have now done a lot of reflecting on your roles in life, your hopes, personal qualities, successes and handicappers. The challenge now is to translate your thinking into goals, plans and actions. This chapter outlines a process for:

- distilling your thinking
- articulating vision and goals
- setting objectives and priorities
- planning to reach your objectives
- making it happen.

The CV is a synthesis of achievements and experience from the past. What you are developing here is an AF, your agenda for the future.

'Dream creative dreams. Set high and worthwhile goals. Take the first decisive step toward your goal. And then what? Take another step, and another, and another, until the goal is reached, the ambition realised, the mission accomplished. No matter what it takes, persist.'

Norman Vincent Peale, American theologian and broadcaster

1. Steps on the way

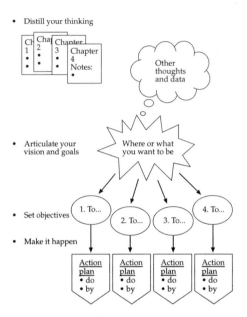

• Distill your thinking

• Articulate your vision and goals

• Set objectives

• Make it happen

2. Distill your thinking

What do you recall as interesting or important from the earlier chapters? Review the chapters if you need to refresh your memory.

? Test Yourself

Summarise the interesting and important points from earlier chapters:

1. Get started
2. Master the monsters
3. Position yourself
4. Inspect the kit

Turn back to when you reflected on why you want to unlock your potential (Chapter 1). You may be starting your first job, or starting a new job. You may be going through a major change in your circumstances , such as divorce or redundancy. You may have reached 40 and realise that you still have half your life left. You know you want it to be different from the first half. Or you may just be asking 'Is that is all there is?'

A great deal of attention is given at school and college to helping young people deal with entry into work and choosing their future area of work. It is now being recognised that people don't complete this process just once. They repeat it with every job change. They will therefore need help with planning their career, not just once at entry into work, but at various points in their working life.

? Test Yourself

Your job/career stage
Which stage are you at?

☐ *Exploration of both self and the world of work.*
Who I am   What I am interested in   What I am good at
What kinds of jobs are out there

☐ *Establishment, settling into an occupation.*
Maybe after some false starts finding a job/career that suits. Making the grade in it, developing within it, making a contribution.

☐ *Maintenance, retaining your position.*
Finding new ways of doing tasks, keeping up to date with changes in work demands and personal goals.

☐ *Disengagement, decreasing involvement.*
Reducing workload, shifting the balance of energy invested in this particular job/career.

Is there any further information or ideas you might want to explore at this point? Would it be helpful to obtain career information from employment agencies, businesses, professional institutes, schools and colleges?

At the age of 16 Mary left school on a Friday. On the Monday she started at the factory where her aunt worked. She really hadn't had any thoughts about what she wanted to do. Her Dad had said the factory was a good opportunity to start earning some money.

Now at the age of 45, with her children grown, Mary had applied to do a counselling course at University College. She wasn't sure what she wanted to do with a counselling diploma but she is now thinking through what some of her options might be.

Distilling your thinking leads you to the next stage – defining your vision and goals.

3. Articulate your vision and goals

What does success mean for you at this time? Chances are it is a very personal view, something that means a lot to you but not to anyone else. Success may also have several meanings for you. Each one is a goal to aim for on the way to fulfilling your potential.

Complete the sentences:
Being successful means …
My dream is to …

This task looks easy, but it isn't or isn't always. You may need to take time to mull it over and to discuss it with those you know and trust. Write your goals out in full.

These are goals that others have set for themselves:
- to have a steady job so I can live a comfortable life with my family.
- to get out of a depression and do something with my life.
- to start up an run a profitable e-commerce business.
- to have a large happy family.
- to downshift to a less stressed, more relaxed lifestyle.

Mary has now been accepted as a mature student in the counselling programme. To celebrate the new direction her life has taken, she treats herself to a makeover at the local beauty salon. Her hair, her wardrobe and her make-up – all transformed. But what she really wants, she thinks afterwards, is an 'internal makeover'. And so she enrols in a life and career development course. Having become aware that her self-esteem is low and 'holding me back', she defines her top goal as improving her self-esteem.

Setting goals is one of the most effective ways of moving yourself forward and achieving what you wish to achieve. But your chances of following this through depend on how much you believe and expect you will succeed. Psychologists call this belief 'self efficacy'. It really means having faith in yourself.

The sense of self efficacy determines:
- whether or not you will attempt something

- how much effort you will put into it, and
- how long you will keep going in the face of difficulties.

You can strengthen the belief in yourself simply by:
- trying – having a go
- watching others who are successful – look for positive role models and learn from them
- seeking encouragement from others – identify people you know can give positive support when you try something new
- avoiding the pessimists.

4. Set objectives and priorities

This section helps you focus on practical and creative ways for accomplishing your goals. These become your objectives. Then you will decide which objectives to work on first.

'Objective setting is "the practicality of eating our elephants one bite at a time", of translating vision into achievable, actionable doing.'
Stephen Covey, educator and business consultant

Psychologists have identified two kinds of thinking that can help you set your objectives.

Divergent thinking is thinking outside of the box – opening up and exploring different directions and possibilities. Divergent thinking means allowing yourself to think outside the normal ways. Open yourself up to new ways and new approaches; say 'why not?' rather than 'why?' Risk making a fool of yourself, being wrong sometimes.

Convergent thinking is thinking inside of the box – finding the right answer or a single best solution. This requires evaluation and judgement.

In the early phase of objective setting, think divergently. In the later stages, think convergently.

Divergent thinking exercises

- Think of 50 uses for a ball-point pen. Be as creative as you can.
- Brainstorm possible options for accomplishing your self-fulfilment goals. Write down as many ideas as you can, however outlandish. Don't cut any of them out as unsuitable. Once that is done go back and sort the ideas into promising, possible and reject categories. Remember to say 'Why Not?' not just 'Why?'

> 'The way to get good ideas is to get lots of ideas and throw the bad ones away.'
> Linus Pauling, American chemist and Nobel Prize winner

When you have finished brainstorming, it is time for convergent thinking. Here is how to judge if an option will make a good objective.

- Setting an objective you are unlikely to achieve is more likely to depress than motivate. So an objective should be challenging. It should stretch you – but it should be attainable.
- Achieving it is *your* responsibility. It needs to be *your* objective, not what someone else thinks you should achieve.

- It should be a positive objective not a negative one. If you tell a youngster not to drop something, what is likely to happen? If instead you say 'hold it steady' the outcome is more likely to be successful.
- It should be SMART – *specific, measurable, attainable, realistic* and *time-bound*.

A SMART objective

After a winter of too much food and too little exercise, Mary has decided to lose weight as one of her self-esteem objectives. This is how she phrased it:

'To lose 5lbs (specific, measurable, attainable and realistic) by June 1st (time-bound.)'

Here is a poorly expressed version: 'I'm going to lose lots of weight soon – I hope.'

?

Test Yourself

Your SMART objectives
- For each goal you have set write out at least two possible objectives that will move you closer to that goal.
- Test each objective against the SMART criteria.

By following some do's and don'ts you can increase your chances of achieving your objectives:

DO

- identify and focus on a few key priorities.
- tell others about your objectives so your commitment is public.

- think of problems as opportunities to learn and to improve your performance.
- establish your own standards and aim to achieve those.

DON'T

- work under such constant pressure that you are chronically short of energy.
- be distracted into non-priority activities.
- let the experience of a setback colour your view of everything.

Imagine yourself standing on a street corner on a windy day. You are clutching a handful of notes: 95 are £5 and 3 are £100 notes. The wind blows them out of your hand. Which of the notes do you chase? Obviously the £100 ones. You need to prioritise your objectives.

?   ## Test Yourself

What are your development priorities?

Which are the £100 objectives – the ones that are most important and where you will see the greatest pay-offs. Complete these sentences.

My £100 objectives are
- To develop . . .
- To change . . .
- To focus on . . .
- To stop . . .
- To start . . .

5. Plan to reach your objectives

Have a written action plan. It will help you:

- define clearly what is to be done, by when and in what order
- anticipate any difficulties or needs that you might otherwise miss
- break down the work into sensibly-sized chunks
- identify where one part of your plan may depend on something else being done first
- spot if you're being diverted and get back on track.

Questions to ask myself

1. What *am* I going to do?
   Not what could I do/am thinking of doing.
2. *When* am I going to do it by?
   Only when I set a time does it become real.
3. What problems/obstacles might I encounter? What kind of support might I need?
4. What has held me back from doing this before? What gets in the way of my good intentions?
5. How certain am I that I *will* actually do it? Give yourself a score out of 10.
6. What do I have to do to make it a score of 10 out of 10?
7. Is the timescale realistic? Does the objective need broken into smaller do-able parts?

Mary has a detailed list of actions each with a start and completion date.

- Read up on low calorie foods
- Walk to work daily
- Don't go by the chip shop
- Weigh herself once weekly
- Celebrate when the target is achieved
- Set new target

Think what success will look like. Imagine yourself with your goal achieved. How will you feel? What will you do? Don't let negative assumptions limit your options for action.

DON'T say

- I can't afford the time
- It can't be done like that
- I'd never be able to do that.

DO ask

- What would I do if I had the time?
- What if I knew the answer? What would it be?
- What would I need to help me do it?

Remember, change of any kind can be uncomfortable and stressful. Even changes you want to make. You are exchanging an old familiar view of yourself for a new and different one. For a while you may feel vulnerable until you have re-established yourself. Sports psychology research shows that successful high performers have something in common. They had to overcome early significant setbacks. Success did not come easy. But it would not have come at all without the learning from those early hard experiences.

> *The Fear Truths*
> 'You can't wait for the fear to go away.
> The fear will never go away as long as you continue to grow.
> The only way to get rid of the fear of doing something is to go out and do it. The doing it comes before the fear goes away.
> The only way to feel better about yourself is to go out...and do it. The doing it comes before the feeling better about yourself.
> Pushing through fear is less frightening than living with the underlying fear that comes from a feeling of helplessness.'
>
> Susan Jeffers, writer and consultant

5. Make it happen

Force field analysis helps to identify what you need to do to achieve your plan. The *field* here is your life situation. It includes external forces (e.g. financial situation and family circumstances) and internal forces (e.g. values and beliefs, self esteem). Whenever you want to make a change there will always be some forces working for you and some working against you.

Steps in a force field analysis:

• define the objective
• list all the forces which help and hinder it

- review your list
- work out how to decrease the negative forces and increase the positive ones
- concentrate on the ideas that will give the biggest pay-off (the long arrows).

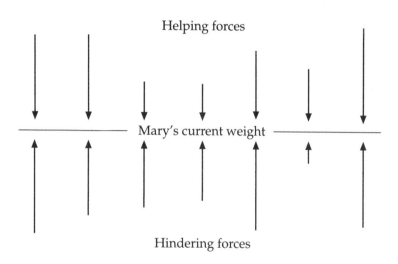

Mary's weight-reduction objective

- Negative forces – sandwich lunches at work, cheese and bread readily available at home
- Positive forces – wanting to look/feel better for holiday in June; paid-up gym membership

- Decreasing the negatives – bring fruit and yoghurt regularly to the office, stop buying bread and cheese in shopping, replace with low-cal things she likes
- Increasing the positives – buy smaller-sized holiday shorts, go with a friend to gym on Tuesdays, stick photo of hotel swimming pool to the fridge door

Warning

Despite your SMART objectives, action plans and good intentions you know deep down that nothing may come of it. Sometimes there are valid practical obstacles. But the biggest reason is your own self imposed limitations! Remember the monsters and myths.

? **Test Yourself**

Monsters and myths
- What self-imposed limitations will affect your development plans?
- Which are related to your class, gender, education or culture?
- Do you want to rid yourself of them?
- How are you going to do it?
- Make it happen.

'The biggest sin is sitting on your ass.'
Florynce Kennedy. Writer and feminist

A critical step: build *progress reviews* into your planning cycle. Before you can set new goals and action plans you need to evaluate what you have achieved, your self esteem and your self-knowledge. But the external world will also be changing. New and different opportunities, challenges and constraints will be emerging. You may need to set new goals to take advantage of these opportunities and to adjust your planning to reflect the new challenges and constraints. This planning and review cycle is forever.

7. The Challenge

- Are you going to do anything different? Name three things.
- Who are you going to tell about your goals, objectives and action commitments?
- When will this happen?
- What are you going to do to avoid self-sabotage?

Travel hopefully

This chapter presents final thoughts for travelling hopefully and successfully:

- going round the U-bend
- the two-wheel learning cycle
- travel companions
- being yourself.

You have been reading in these pages about exploring, risk-taking, experiencing, discovering, perfecting, self-developing, being vulnerable. All ingredients of the learning process and all essential to fulfilling your potential. In practice people don't think a lot about their learning. They just do whatever it is they are doing and some of the experience sticks. This is not always effective learning and this chapter explains why.

> 'Experience has given us some of our finest flute players. Experience has also given us some of our worst flute players.'
>
> Plato

1. Going round the U-bend

When people talk about the learning curve they are usually thinking of this one.

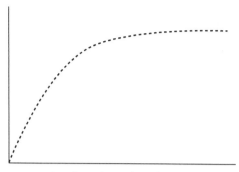

The learning curve is often found in the controlled laboratory experiments carried out by psychologists. It has an intuitive appeal. It promises that skill proficiency and knowledge will increase with experience and training. A moment's refection reminds us that real life is rather more complex. What often happens in practice is that things get *worse* before they get better. Remember 'two-steps-forward-one-back' (Chapter 1)? Think back to a time when you were learning a new and difficult skill, or mastering a new job. The process and the script might have looked something like this.

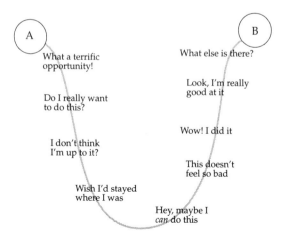

Simply knowing you are likely to go down before you come up gives hope and encouragement. You can persevere through the 'bad times' if you know that competence will eventually come.

2. The two-wheel learning cycle

There are two processes at work when you go down then up the U-bend. One is a cognitive cycle which is steered by the *executive self* (Chapter 2). Your rational mind is actively focusing, attending, memorizing, recalling and executing.

The other learning cycle, mainly emotional, involves self-esteem in a big way. You experience feelings – anxiety, discomfort, anger – that can be uncomfortable and threatening. And you need to handle those threats to protect your self esteem. Both wheels have to work in tandem if you are to get around and up that curve.

Here is how the cognitive process works when you are learning efficiently and effectively. Start at step 1.

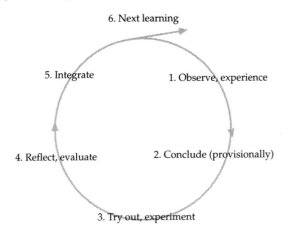

6. Next learning

5. Integrate

1. Observe, experience

4. Reflect, evaluate

2. Conclude (provisionally)

3. Try out, experiment

The process of cognitive learning is very *aware*. (1) You participate in a situation, or you see or hear something. (2) Next you mull it over. You analyse what happened when, why and how. You draw hypotheses and arrive at provisional conclusions. (3) Then you seek out opportunities to test the conclusions. (4) You evaluate the trial and finally (5) integrate the learning into your *self knowledge*. Consciously planning and using experience in these deliberate ways produces powerful learning.

At other times you seem to get stuck on the downward slope of the U-bend. How many times have you set out to improve yourself and didn't follow through? Or master an instrument, take a course, study a book? Have you ever resolved to take on board critical feedback and done precisely nothing? Do course handouts gather dust on your shelves? How about those resolutions to quit smoking, lose weight, become fitter?

You get stuck because learning requires change and changing is hard to do. It is easier to stay as you are. Learning also has opportunity costs – to spend less time with family or friends, putting away the golf clubs, giving up a holiday. And emotion can totally sabotage your learning.

Emotions and learning

Take a moment to picture in your mind a situation in which you had to learn something new. Maybe a new job, or a software package, or playing golf for the first time. How did you feel when you started out? Excited, keen, confident, competent? How about uncomfortable, anxious, incompetent? Frustrated? A bit silly?

Here is what happens when your emotions sabotage learning.

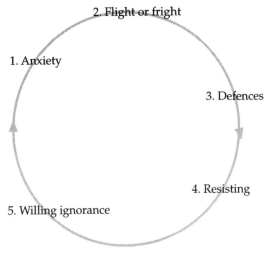

2. Flight or fright

1. Anxiety

3. Defences

4. Resisting

5. Willing ignorance

1. *Anxiety.* Certain aspects of learning arouse anxiety and emotional discomfort. It feels like being a child again and subservient. Difficulty with learning assails your sense of being a competent person. A newly learned skill is clumsy and feels unnatural. It looks contrived to others (you think). Your cherished beliefs may have to be discarded and old behaviour changed. Feelings like these pose a threat to your self-esteem.

2. *Fight or flight.* Threats to self-esteem, if serious enough, provoke instinctive gut reactions. You freeze, you walk out of the situation or you become aggressive. People became tongue-tied in class. They turn down promotions. They go off to the pub when they ought to be studying. They throw the book in the trash can. They get into heated arguments with the instructor. We each have our own favoured gut reaction.

3. *Defences*. People have well-practiced mechanisms to defend against such strong emotions. Denial, rationalising and avoidance are the main ones. 'It isn't all that important'. 'More important things to do.' 'Spend quality time with the children.' 'I need a life.' 'No will power.' 'This stuff is academic, it's not real.' 'Smoking doesn't cause cancer.' Sound familiar?

4. *Resisting*. The more you avoid the challenge of learning, the more you resist. *Even when it is manifestly in their best interest*, resisters remain firmly committed to the past ('the good old days', 'the old ways are good enough for me'). Resistance to learning new things and different ways can be observed in organisations undergoing change.

5. *Willing ignorance*. When rooted in emotional experience, resistance is 'irrational' and immune to rational argument. You become even *less* willing to expose yourself to risk. Non-learning becomes a way of life. Hence the continuing state of willing ignorance.

Here is how to work through these blocks in the learning process.

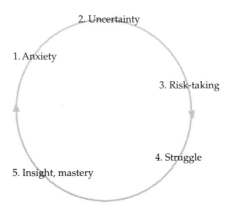

1. *Anxiety*. Acknowledge your uncomfortable feelings: they are absolutely normal. Think back to your memories and the unpleasant feelings associated with learning. Knowing that such emotions are common and entirely normal helps to alleviate them. Anticipate the positive emotional pay-off from successful learning – confidence, pride, relief, self-esteem. Re-instate the *executive controller* (Chapter 2). Break the learning task into smaller do-able pieces. Eat the elephant one bite at a time.

2. *Uncertainty*. Uncertainty arises when you are not sure if you will learn. 'Will I succeed?' It arises when your anxiety, fear and anger come head-to-head with an internal voice saying 'learning is good for you'. It comes about when you feel your sense of who you are being challenged.
There are several counter-measures. Be very clear about your learning goal – what you aim to achieve. Create a positive vision in your mind's eye – what it will be like, how good it will feel when you have learned. Keep referring to your goal, your vision, your inspiration to fulfil your potential. Accept your anxiety and other emotions as real but don't punish yourself for experiencing them. Accept that you may change a belief or a behaviour, but you remain the same whole person.

3. *Risk-taking*. We have spoken already about taking calculated risks. Keep yourself well informed in the area where you are taking the risk. Avoid leaping into the unknown. Weigh up the options and their costs/benefits. Find low-risk situations, such as training courses, to experiment with new behaviours. Seek the opinions of those who are informed. Bring people into your confidence. If you are experimenting with a different

style for leading others, tell them what you are trying to do and why. Ask for their feedback and support.

4. *Struggle.* Continue to think of potential as a process not a state (Chapter 1). Remember: two steps forward one step back. Accept that backsliding is normal but it doesn't have to be permanent. Be sure to celebrate small successes along the way. Form a self-help group or an action-learning group. You can do this on the internet as well as face-to-face. Learning in a group gives a lot of mutual support. Find a coach, mentor, or group facilitator who understands the emotional side of learning. Remain in control of *your* learning, and take responsibility for it.

5. *Insight, mastery.* Make a habit of it. Celebrate every success.

?

Test Yourself

Breaking out of the negative loop
- Have you personal experiences of the negative emotional wheel? How did you break out of it? What has worked for you?
- Reflecting on the positive emotional wheel, what practical steps can you take from it to apply to your learning?

'Top performers ask a further question: 'What do I need to learn?' They don't waste time berating themselves for doing something badly. They look for shortfalls that impede their use of strengths, and for corrections ... From 'What do I need to learn?' comes a variety of follow-ups. 'What am I doing that I should do more of? That I should cut down? In what areas do

I need to improve? What is the most effective way to get up to speed?'

Garfield, author and management guru

3. Travel companions

We say again: this is a personal journey, only you can unlock your potential. But we are social beings and relationships are vital. Imagine yourself 800 years ago. You aspire to be a master-builder of the wonderful cathedrals of that era. In pursuit of your craft you journey from one site to the next, not alone but in the company of a master (journeyman) stonemason. Walking together, you speak of your dreams and aspirations, you learn from his wisdom and guidance. A bond of trust and confidence joins you.

Have friends and supporters by your side. Find a mentor to walk with as you develop your potential. More than one if you can and especially when you are going through a major transition. The acid test is someone to whom you can reveal yourself and not regret it later.

The various members of Mary's network give her support in different ways, social, emotional and practical. Her relationships cut both ways. She gives as well as receives, which is an essential feature of good networks.

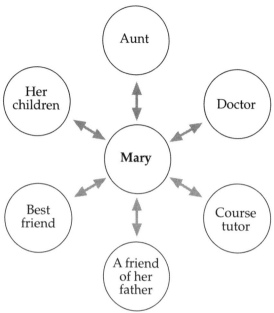

Mary's support network

Being healthy and fit is one of the areas for fulfilment we explored (Chapter 3). Simon is our GP working in a busy practice. His knowledge and medical competence are second to none. But what really distinguishes him is the respect, care and mutuality he brings to his practice. Simon has the gift of being positively helpful without diminishing the sense of responsibility for our own well-being.

? **Test Yourself**

Your support network
- Draw a map of the people you can count on for support.
- In one or two words describe what you get from the relationship.
- In one or two words describe what you give to the relationship.
- Are there other relationships you can explore?

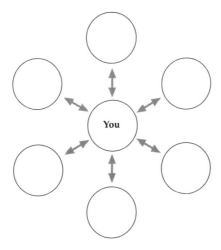

Quality is more important than the number of 'travel companions' you have. You will get more from, and give more to, a small number of good relationships than many superficial ones.

Relationships are not always smooth sailing. You need to work at them.

DO

- Give the relationship your time and attention.

- Explain what support you would find helpful.
- Ask for feedback – be specific.
- Accept feedback gracefully, the negative kind as well as positive.
- Give thanks.
- Relationships are two-way – recognize and respond to the other person's needs.
- Be prepared to disagree – being agreeable doesn't mean you always agree.
- Listen – be prepared to change your mind.

DON'T
- Take the relationship for granted.
- Ask for ready-made solutions – devise your own.
- Put yourself down or constantly apologise – this turns people off.
- Discount compliments and positive feedback.
- Defer to others just to please them.
- Fudge or be vague about how you feel and where you stand.

In all areas – family, work, religion, entertainment, education, politics – membership of communities and groups provides many opportunities to fulfil your potential and expand it. Undertaking unfamiliar roles, taking on new responsibilities, contributing to work groups and task forces – all are learning opportunities. Being in a group offers unique learning: how people from different gender and backgrounds think and feel; insights from dialogue and sharing experiences; exploring and discovering things together; feedback from other members. To make the most of these opportunities, remember the U-bend and the learning cycle.

Being yourself

Unlocking your potential is truly being yourself and having faith to be yourself. Faith gives you confidence to make choices. Choosing to live in the light and out of the shadows. Choosing a success-goal that is right for you at this time of your life. Choosing what to learn, what to practice. Unlocking your potential is a full-time job. You need to be doing it all the time you are relating to others, while you are working, and during study, play and prayer. But think of the pay-off!

Some final suggestions, some repeated:

DO

- Be forgiving of yourself.
- Be aware of your emotions – accept them and enjoy them.
- Talk to yourself, tell yourself how good you are.
- Set a daily goal for something you will achieve.
- Keep a journal listing of what went well – an accomplishment, a conflict settled, a friendship strengthened, a kindness from someone, a compliment.
- Re-read your notes when your feelings are low.
- Be positive in your words: look for the glass that is half-full, not half-empty.
- Find a daily opportunity to pay others a genuine compliment.
- Accept that your needs and feelings are as important as other people's.
- Be who *you* want to be.

DON'T

- Beat yourself up.
- Talk yourself down.
- Set impossibly high standards, or ones that are too low.
- Do negative introspection – it stops you changing.
- Dwell on the world's problems.
- Try to be what others want you to be.

From 'A friendship blessing'

'May you learn to be a good friend to your self.
May you be able to journey to that place in your soul
where there is great love, warmth, feeling and
forgiveness.
May this change you.
May it transfigure that which is negative, distant or cold
in you.
May you be brought into the real passion, kinship and
affinity of belonging.'

John O'Donohue, poet and scholar

The challenge

DO IT.

Sources and references

Introduction: Unlock your potential

Maslow, A. A theory of human motivation. *Psychological Review*, 1943, Vol. 50. No. 4.
Robert Heller, *Management Today*, 1982.

Chapter 2: Master the monsters

For a scholarly but readable treatment of the self, refer to readings in Roy F. Baumeister (Ed.) *The Self in Social Psychology*. Philadelphia: Psychology Press, 1999.

To find out more about transactional analysis and 'drivers': Stewart, I. and Joines, V. *TA Today*. Nottingham, UK and Chapel Hill, North Carolina USA: Lifespace Publishing, 1987.
Wagner, A. *The Transactional Manager*. London: The Industrial Society, 1996.

For more about locus of control:
Rotter, J.B. Internal versus external control of reinforcement: A case history of a variable. *American Psychologist*, 45, 489–493.

Dweck, C.S. *Self-Theories*. Philadelphia: Psychology Press, 2000.
Bennis, W. and Nanus, B. *Leaders*. New York: Harper & Row, 1985.

Chapter 3: Position yourself

Langer, E. *Mindfulness*. London: Harvill/Harper-Collins, 1989.

Levinson, D.J., Darrow, C.N., Klein, E.B., Levinson, M.H., McKee, B. *The Seasons of a Man's Life*. New York: Knopf, 1978.

For excellent ideas on how to find learning opportunities see:
Lombardo, M.M. and Eichinger, R.W *Eighty-Eight Assignments for Development in Place*. Center for Creative Leadership, Greensboro, North Carolina, 1989.
Although written for managers, non-managers can profitably adapt the material.

Chapter 4: Inspect your kit

O'Donohue, J. *Anam Cara*. London: Bantam Books, 1999.
Gardner, H. *Frames of Mind*. London: Heinemann, 1984.

For a scholarly, research-based but readable account of fixed and flexible theories of intelligence, the authoritative source is:
Dweck, C.S. *Self-Theories.* Philadelphia: Psychology Press, 2000.

To find out more about personality and psychological assessment:
Furnham, A. and Heaven, P. *Personality and Social Behaviour*. London: Arnold – Hodder, 1999.
Kline, P. *The Handbook of Psychological Testing.* Routledge, 1993.

Chapter 5: Make it happen

Peale, N.V. *The Plus Factor.* London: Cedar-Heinemann, 1987.
Covey, S.R., Merrill, A.R. and Merrill, R. *First Things First.* New York: Fireside/Simon & Schuster, 1994.

Jeffers, S. *Feel the Fear and Do It Anyway.* London: Century Hutchinson, 1987.

Chapter 6: Travel hopefully

The two-wheel cycle builds on the original insights of: Vince, R. and Martin, L. Inside action learning: an exploration of the psychology and politics of the action learning model. *Management Education and Development*, Vol. 24, Part 3, 1993.
Garfield, C. *Peak Performers.* New York: Avon Books, 1987.
O'Donohue, J. see earlier reference.

Some useful websites
www.bbc.co.uk/education/workskills/careerlinks/shtml
www.careersolutions.co.uk